GIOCONDO BOCCIARELLI

Topics of Theory of Neurosciences II: Conditioning, Behavior, Emotions and Love

The author is a doctor specialized in neurology at the University Hospital of Perugia, Italy, where he works in the Emergency Department.
He has a special interest in theory of neurosciences.

E.mail: _giocondobocciarelli@ymail.com_

ISBN   978-1-291-98289-3

PREFACE

This work of research tackles topics that are thought too large and complicated, but I have focused on some key problems and have achieved some answers.

The models are described in a clear and simple style, but also synthetic and unorthodox. Some passages are very difficult to understand without a various and particular background (and an open mind too...).

The chapter I, about conditioning, comes from an article concluded in 1993, that was presented to various professors and journals, but rejected and never published up to now.

The chapter II, about behavior, was completed in 1995 and presented to many journals and professors, but rejected.

The chapter III, about emotions, was completed in 2005, presented to various journals and professors, but always rejected.

Afterwards I put together these two last articles as the chapter I and the chapter II of the book *Topics of Theories of Neurosciences: Behavior and Emotions* that I published myself in 2008.

The chapter IV, about love, is totally new, presented and published only here for the first time.

So this book has the similar title of the predecessor and includes all my four works of study on theory of neurosciences. They are together to be evidence of the evolution of these researches and their coherence and interlinking. Moreover the first chapters were left unmodified to verify them with the development of the disciplines.

G.B.

I am profoundly grateful to some Persons that supported me and were very patient with me during the long times of elaborating these ideas, especially the most difficult ones.
      Thanks!
Giocondo

CONTENTS

GENERAL INTRODUCTION

In the absurd event of an ancient Roman reappearing on the Earth today, and meeting then a car, he would probably look at it with wonder, and he would call it by a different way, perhaps *carrus sine equo* ("cart without horse"). But the question of definitions, being at first nominalistic, becomes central as one tries to spot some great functions and their corresponding frames. One of the features of this "carrus", for instance, is that of moving and reducing its speed so much that it comes to a stop. But if our Roman does not master the concepts of deceleration due to lowering of power (decrease of fuel), and to internal (e.g. brakes) or external (e.g. going uphill) resistance, he would finally say, for instance, that it stopped only because the hill; whereas deceleration may have been due also to the other causes. Therefore his calculations upon part of the observed phenomena are not going to be right, and he will often draw some distorted general conclusions. Or else, if he thought it is only the accelerator that accelerates and decelerates the car, he would not discriminate the wheels' braking system, and he would consider it as linked to the same wheel without any particular distinct function or mixed with other systems! Nevertheless the wheel has several well distinguished structural subsets (suspension, axle shaft, brakes, tires), and each of them has very definite functions (bearing, stabilizing, propellant, braking, steering...).

All this underlines to us how little mistakes in a general definition put seriously off the track particular hypotheses and a great number of those experiments based on that system. As an instance, we may here mention the thin and yet enormous difference in defining force between Aristotelian and Galilean mechanics: $f=mv$ changes in $f=ma$! We can imagine what is nowadays happening to us on such a complex subject like the "brain-mind" system.

I. CONDITIONING: OVERCOMING THE TWO-TYPE THEORIES

Introduction

The division between classical and instrumental conditioning reflects the viewing of a single phenomenon from two different secondary standpoints. Nevertheless, the stimulus-response model is too simple to be used effectively in the analysis of conditioning phenomena.

Skinner (1935) first suggested a clear four-term model for conditioning, which, to avoid confusion, can be described as:

$$cS > cR \ > \ uS > uR$$

(S = Stimulus; R = Response;
c = conditioned; u = unconditioned)

and which he later modified according to the types of conditioning that he classified. In practice, in classical conditioning only the part cS > uS was valid; in operant conditioning only cR > uS; in discriminative conditioning only cS > cR > uS (Skinner, 1938).

Later theories emphasized this difference on the basis of the principles of contiguity and of reinforcement (cf. Mowrer, 1947; Rescorla and Solomon, 1967).

Then, these principles were reconsidered by the following experiments and theories: the experiments of Garcia, Ervin and

Koelling (1966), the blocking effect of Kamin (1968), the theory of Rescorla and Wagner (1972) and the omission training of Gormezano and Coleman (1973).

Finally, the currently accepted "two-type" theories of conditioning are based on the principle of contingency: stimulus-stimulus contingency (cS-uS) in classical conditioning, i.e. the unconditioned stimulus will occur if, and only if, the conditioned stimulus first occurs, regardless of "the animal's behavior"; the response-stimulus contingency (cR-uS) in instrumental conditioning, i.e. the unconditioned stimulus occurs if, and only if, the conditioned response occurs (see Mackintosh, 1983, p. 77).

Here the behavioristic analysis has reached its apex and no more can be said by it simply because it ignores the mind, whereas now it is necessary to deal also with it, in order to discover completely the mechanism of conditioning. In fact some authors have already used new perspectives in observing these phenomena, e.g. the adaptationist-ethological approach of Staddon (1983) and the little more cognitivistic one of Rescorla (1988).

In practice, a better definition of this mechanism will result only from an accurate and complete analysis of the factors in the behavior process during conditioning.

1) A new model of the conditioning process

It will not be attempted here to reduce one model to another, as was often done, but rather a complete and integrated model will be delineated by taking into account, as far as possible, the complexity of the process, and by including the essential factors and phases of both types of paradigms:

$$\left\{ pS \rightarrow \begin{array}{c} psR \\ \\ pvR \end{array} \right\}_n \rightarrow \left\{ fS \rightarrow \begin{array}{c} fsR \\ \\ fvR \end{array} \right\}_n$$

(S = Stimulus; R = Response; s = skeletal; v = visceral; p = preparatory; f = final; n = ordinal number)

The *visceral responses* regard the internal organs e.g., heart, arteries, glands etc. The *skeletal responses* concern the striated muscles. The fS is the *reward* which means satisfying a need of the subject. It can be "appetitive effective", when it is pleasant and given (e.g. the food in the bowl); or "aversive omissive", when it is unpleasant and is removed (e.g. the shock is eliminated). On the other hand, especially at the beginning of the process, a pS (stimulus of preparatory cycle) can be a *punishment* because it is associated with a sense of dissatisfaction. It can be "appetitive omissive", when it is pleasant but absent, e.g. lack of food; or "aversive effective" when it is unpleasant and exists, e.g. applying shock (cf.

Skinner, 1953).

Cycle, as used here, is the association of a stimulus to skeletal and visceral responses, and is the basic unit of the process. The subject's skeletal and visceral activity occur at the same time. Moreover there are some *preparatory cycles* which vary according to the environmental situation and in which learning occurs. It is characterized by a sense of dissatisfaction for a need. There are also *final cycles* which are fixed and conclude the process. The *ordinal number* of every cycle indicates its temporal sequence and changes during the course of the experiment, because some cycles can be shifted around, repeated or eliminated.

The important thing is to regard learning as a process whose conditions change from beginning to end. During the process, the individual tries to select the most effective, easiest and quickest *path*, i.e. a sequence of n cycles, until the final cycle (fS-fR) is reached and the need satisfied.

Optimization of the process is obtained by adding new cycles and removing others which, at the end of the process, turn out to be incorrect (i.e. those which lead the subject further from the reward) or superfluous, even though they might have been initially useful. Good cycles are not eliminated but speeded up, and their accuracy and frequency are increased, but the path is always a complete one, because certain cycles are indispensable.

If the individual does not find different solutions, or is not stimulated to do so, then cycles and paths can be set up that are either unnecessary, inaccurate, erroneous or hurtful. This will be considered in the section 3 - "Some critical phenomena".

Finally, learning, and thus conditioning too, must be explained in an adaptationist perspective. An individual, when faced with problematic stimuli, must find some responses that can satisfy his need, by removing the stimuli that have a negative valence and by making his own those which have a positive one.

2) The traditional paradigms of conditioning

In light of the previous model, the following paradigms can be reinterpreted: the fundamental experiments of Pavlov (1927) with dogs, and those of Skinner (1938) with rats in boxes equipped with a lever, and also those using a maze; as well as those in which a rat has to jump from one compartment of a shuttle box to the other to avoid getting shocked.

First of all we have to underline the importance of an *exact identification of the factors* acting in each experience. A law is not totally right if it ignores one or more essential factors of the phenomenon, or identifies them in a wrong manner. Thus, in the classical paradigm, at the end of the process, the pS1 is the sound of a bell; the psR1, the turning of the animal's head towards the food dispenser; the pS2, the seeing of the food; the psR2, the grasping of it; the fS, the food being in its mouth; the fsR, the chewing of it; and the fvR is salivation. In Konorski's classical paradigm (Miller and Konorski, 1928) the psR is leg bending. In the instrumental paradigm of Skinner the pS is the seeing of the lever and the psR the pressing of it. In the discriminative paradigm the pS are two or more stimuli to be selected by the psR.

Then it must be emphasized the *complexity of responses and stimuli* and the *adaptive perspective of the behavior process* in which conditioning is carried out. Although it is clear that only some parameters can be used to collect data about learning, there are many elements that are involved in this process. The skeletal response and the visceral one are integrated and combined into a single, greater response. Moreover both of them are made up of many elementary ones, which are the activation of a certain muscle or organ. A simple reflex, such as withdrawing a hand from a hot stove, must be seen in the context of a more complex behavior related to fear. Conversely, some elements of a complex behavior can be used in a particular learning phenomenon, e.g., a dog's food-begging behavior applied in the Pavlovian conditioning of salivation (cf. Zener, 1937; Lorenz, 1981, p. 297; Timberlake and Lucas, 1989).

Furthermore the preparatory responses always respond to certain *stimuli* (pS), at times generic, but always necessary and present, e.g. the box itself, which is a valid and powerful stimulus. At other times the stimuli are better defined and similar to each other, e.g. when a rat is between two different levers only one of which is positively reinforcing. Thus hearing the bell and seeing the lever are functionally equivalent.

The reward (fS) cannot be substituted by a previous preparatory stimulus (pS), but during learning a particular preparatory stimulus (pS1) can replace another subsequent one (pS2). For example, in an experiment in which a bell preannounces a shock, the response of fleeing is first to the shock and then to the bell. But to complete the process, the reward, e.g. the state of well-being, must always be present. On the other hand, the preparatory stimuli that have a punitive valence tend to be eliminated.

The *visceral responses* occur with the skeletal ones in all the paradigms, as is also true of the rat in Skinner's experiment. These factors are necessary as well. The dog in the Pavlovian paradigm certainly associates the previously neutral new stimulus with salivating, but this is a secondary and closely linked phenomenon. The essential point is that it has learned the path which leads to eating in that particular environmental setting, otherwise it will not even salivate.

Moreover it is not possible to compare different types of responses with each other. In the Pavlovian conditioning only visceral responses are generally taken into consideration, while the skeletal ones are ignored. The opposite takes place in an asymmetrical manner in instrumental conditioning. In addition, only responses that exist at the same stage of the process must be compared. For example, salivation is a visceral response and is part of the final cycle, whereas pressing the lever is a skeletal one and part of a preparatory cycle. But salivation must occur in both the dog and the rat at the same learning phase and stage (see the experiment with dogs of Shapiro, 1960).

In addition, during learning, when a subsequent stimulus is very probable, visceral responses may occur just before the corresponding skeletal ones. This is to favor the carrying out of skeletal responses since they are elements of a single, greater response, e.g., salivating and chewing, erection and coitus, tachycardia and flight, etc. Moreover, some fR can overflow towards a sure pS, e.g., the rats which lick a lever associated to milk as reward (see Davey, Phillips and Cleland, 1981).

By considering *the difference between respondent and instrumental responses*, the interpretations of the paradigms are dual and opposite, and thus are contradictory and cancel each other out.

With regard to the avoidance behavior as in a standard shuttle box, if flight is seen as a simple reflexive response to pain, then, if the animal flees on hearing a sound, we have an example of classical conditioning. But its flight does not involve manipulating anything. Nevertheless this experiment is usually classified as instrumental conditioning, because the rat must jump from one compartment to another and this response is instrumental in avoiding the shock.

In the case of a maze we can interpret what occurs as follows: (1) if a rat runs along the correct path, it receives food, and this is instrumental conditioning; (2) if a rat acquires a series of correct stimuli, it is offered food and then it salivates, and this is classical conditioning.

A dog's lifting of its leg, as in Kornorski's paradigm (Miller and Konorski, 1928), would be classified as an instrumental response. But the dog does not manipulate the environment. Yet, can moving a part of its own body not be considered a true instrumental response?

In practice, the subsequent skeletal response is the one that is respondent to a certain stimulus, but at the same time brings the reward nearer, or seems to, and therefore is instrumental.

The *preparatory skeletal responses* (psR) are the ones that lead the animal to getting the reward (fS) and they are always present. In Pavlov's classical paradigm, a dog is restrained by a harness and presumed to be passive. In fact it cannot move around and obtains food without effort on its part. After having learned that it must remain still (since the problem of escape is, so to speak, solved by being suppressed), the dog has to provide for another need, namely hunger. Thus it tries to satisfy this by performing several responses, like jumping, turning its head in various directions, etc. First, this is done randomly and then in a more controlled way as it discovers the solution to the problem of how to nourish itself.

The new response learned by the dog during this process is very important and should be noted. It must remain still and wait for a particular sound; at which point it must direct its eyes (and its head, and its body too, if necessary and possible) towards the specific place where food will be given. Failure to do this, e.g. turning in the wrong direction, will not allow it to achieve the objective and will not even result in salivation. Therefore, the psR are always present in this paradigm too (cf. Spence, 1956, pp. 160-163).

As with the rat in Skinner's box, a number of *n* trials are also necessary for the dog to achieve conditioning by selecting the right cycles. The fact that the dog is harnessed, even though does not eliminate the preparatory phase, does, however, make the process easier, since food is placed right under its nose. On the other hand, consider the situation with Skinner's box, where the right stimulus is in the form of a lever that is always available in most experiments. But this does not elicit attentive responses (see below) as effectively as sound does. So the rat can make many possible responses (jumping, turning its head in various directions, scratching, rasping, biting etc.), but most of them result in failure. For an exact comparison it would be necessary to harness the rat and place it in front of the lever, and under such conditions learning would be quicker.

Having demonstrated that skeletal preparatory responses are always present, the only clear distinction that can be made is between elementary *intransitive* and *transitive responses*, according to the following meanings. The former regard only the sense organs or the body in itself (e.g., moving its eyes, staring, jumping, turning the head, moving around), whereas the latter require either little or a lot of direct intervention on the environment in an attempt to modify objects in it (e.g., lever pressing, biting, manipulating to break or displace, etc.). According to this definition the skeletal responses in the maze trials and jumping in the shuttle box are intransitive. Although the distinction between intransitive and transitive responses is important for the individual involved, it is secondary and misleading as far as an analysis of the process is concerned.

In practice up to now this theoretical point has remained the crux of the problem of a false significant separation between two types of conditioning. Contrary to Kimble, "The original distinction between instrumental and classical conditioning is made on purely operational grounds. The two designations refer respectively to training procedures in which the response of the subject does or does not determine whether the UCS appears" (Kimble, 1961, p. 78), also at the operational level we cannot introduce this difference. In fact the important thing is that in the environment there are always two events that are regularly contingent on each other. In the first case they depend on each other with the individual's intervention on them, while in the second case it is not needed. With Kimble, the UCS (reward) must appear, but appear to whom? To the experimenter or to the subject? Also in the second case the individual has to do something in order to make this association his own, otherwise it is a phenomenon far removed from him, and thus is of no use to him. The fact that the subject can obtain more reward in some cases of the first type is not due to another mechanism of learning but to the reinforcement's schedule applied in that particular experience.

Moreover in this framework one finds justification for the "*attentive responses*" which are intransitive psR elicited by an unexpected and salient variation of the environment, and which cause the subject to concentrate better on potentially useful stimuli (cf. "orienting reflex", Pavlov, 1927; "observing responses", Wychoff, 1952). This process can be described as follows: (1) S1 = the lever is glimpsed; (2) R1 = the individual turns towards the lever and focuses on it; (3) S2 = the lever is seen; finally (4) R2 = the lever is pressed.

Thus, it can be concluded that in the conditioning process,

by way of a response, an individual interacting with his environment acquires a contingency between two events (S1-R-S2). In addition, along with these, there are some secondary principles, e.g., generalization, reinforcement schedules, intervals, etc. which obviously are unique for all the paradigms and have been already well studied.   They are not the mechanism of conditioning but they establish its parameters.

3) Some critical phenomena

In the history of psychological literature on this issue, the main obstacles to a "one-type" theory have been represented by the following paradigms.

In the **autoshaping** experiment of Brown and Jenkins (1968) a pigeon obtains food after unnecessary pecking, however solving the problem and becoming adapted to the environment. Pecking is a reflexive response to lights but here it is not incorrect, it is only excessive and not optimal. If there is no stimulation to change (e.g., imitation, punishment of response), why should it modify its behavior? At the end of the learning process the important thing is that some new useful connections (cycles and paths) have been formed, even if some old ones may remain. Another example is the dog in a Pavlovian paradigm that reacts by looking first at the bell and then at the food bowl (see Zener, 1937).

"Omissive-autoshaping" (Williams and Williams, 1969; Atnip, 1977) demonstrated that learning occurred. The percentage of incorrect responses (i.e. pecking at the light) per trials is under 30, thus if pecking does not achieve the desired reward the action is not repeated.   Certainly pecking is a species-specific response to lights (cf. Seligman, 1970), and

therefore this cycle demonstrates a strong tendency to be carried out, but also this behavior can be inhibited if it becomes ineffective. The question is quantitative, depending on the value of the parameters (intertrial interval, reinforcement schedule, etc.) that permit the individual to discriminate the right behavior under different conditions (cf. Jenkins, Barnes and Barrera, 1981; Picker, Grossett, Thomas and Poling, 1984). If these parameters are not clear, they sustain a moderate ratio of "wrong" responses because animal behavior becomes uncertain and more variable.

"Appetitive omission training". To begin with, Sheffield's statement in his paper (1965, p. 306), "the omission procedure outlined above in which from the standpoint of the law of effect, the dog is rewarded with food whenever he fails to salivate to tone...", is in my opinion incorrect. A hungry animal cannot be asked not to salivate at the sight of food which it is sure to get and in a short amount of time. Neither does a dog salivate because "he learns that salivating improves the taste of the food" (Mackintosh, 1983, p. 26). The biological aim of salivation is clear and evident, but it is not learned. As was seen above, salivation is an elementary visceral response (fvR) associated to the skeletal response (fsR) of chewing, that form together the great final response of eating. Thus the dog associates the sound with the final response (fR) of eating, and not only with salivation!

Indeed the dog in Sheffield's experiment does not learn how not to salivate (it does it only at a low ratio) since the parameters are ambiguous. The dog's task is to remain still and wait for the onset of the preparatory stimulus (pS, the tone) and then, only after an additional 4 seconds, does it eat. Biologically an animal always salivates just before eating, and so a "well-practiced" animal tends to perform the response in proximity to the reward (fS, possessing the food). But in this case the reward is too near the pS and the animal gets ready to eat immediately after the onset of pS. So salivation sometimes falls into the critical interval. Thus some trials are good (it gets the food) and others are not, and the pS becomes very ambiguous. It is easier for the dog to discover the right solution if the interval between pS and fS is longer. This was confirmed by Shapiro and Herenden's experiment (1975) who found that if dogs are in the presence of noise for 10 seconds before obtaining food, then they wait the same amount of time before salivating.

In Coleman's experiment of *"aversive omission training"* (1975) there were 4 groups named 5-5, 5-3, 5-1 and 5-0: the first digit indicates the size of the electric shock given off if the desired conditioned response (nictitating membrane extension within 0.4 seconds from the tone onset) does not occur, whereas the second digit indicates this size if the conditioned response takes place. The rabbits' problem is to eliminate the shock that, at a particular level of intensity, causes a typical physiological reaction of defense and flight. But this preparatory response is not entirely carried out because the animal is confined to the experimental box, and it is expressed only by a few visceral responses like that of the nictitating membrane.

For the groups 5-5, 5-3 and 5-1 (the "classical group") this response occurs immediately and strongly in a tragic and mistaken attempt to force the situation, because the shock cannot be avoided. They are highly motivated and there is no other solution. In group 5-0 (the "omission group"), on the other hand, the rabbits can sometimes, although at first only randomly, respond correctly and thus avoid the shock. They are less excited and try to discover the interval (0.4 seconds) within which they can have the reward. Then their longer latency and lower amplitude are noted. Hence, this group does not show the best performance, but demonstrates good learning and adaptation (80 per cent of the right pR at asymptote). Whereas groups 5-5, 5-3, 5-1 seem to reach a very high level of learning, but only by chance, because of the impossibility of avoiding the shock: no adaptation is achieved and the process is not completed (cf. Seligman and Maier, 1967).

Finally, we have to analyze *the effects of **partial reinforcement** upon "the two forms" of conditioning* (see Kimble, 1961, pp. 103-104). In short, in a procedure in which the reward (food) is not given every trial, the classical response of a dog (e.g. salivation) is hardly learned, whereas the operant response is often performed. In reality, when the conditions are equal learning occurs at the same time (see Shapiro, 1960). In fact we have not to confuse a final cycle (e.g. salivation), which occur only when food is sure, with many preparatory cycles (e.g., turning the head, pressing the lever), which the subject may effect many times in the hope of some good outcomes.

Conclusions

Unfortunately the theoretical problem regarding the types of conditioning has not been solved, but only put aside. In fact this error has been taken up again, this time by modern cognitivistic theorists, like Amsel also confirms (1992, p. 338), todays there are "Pavlovian cognitivists" as well as "Skinnerian cognitivists"! In the history of psychology, important schools of thought, never totally correct however, have often tried to absorb and redefine the positive part of the competing theories on the basis of their own terms and methods. In practice, by denying the positive and negative parts of each others theories, the development of a complete and integrated science of learning has been hampered.

However, in contrast to Amsel, the main underlying problem still exists and should not be dismissed as unreal or of no consequence. Learning, as a cognitivist like Bara (1990, p. 152) asserts, is a key phenomenon of mental activity which is at the center of faculties like memory, motivation and intelligence. The most important schools of thought in psychology have had to compare and contrast their ideas with this problem, even though it was not their main field of investigation. He states, moreover, that success has been partial and unsatisfying, but once this problem is solved, others linked to it will disappear. Yet, as was said in the introduction, behaviorism cannot furnish us with a clear, complete and significant theory of learning, as Hull (1943) tried to do.

Only in the light of a clear definition and a right model of conditioning, we will be able to attack the problem of an integrated view of the behavior mechanism. Then, also in order to explain better our model, we can turn to the topic of emotion, which continues, among other thing, to constitute the basis of the modern two-process theory of conditioning (see Domjan, 1993, chap. 10).

II. A GENERAL INTEGRATED THEORY OF BEHAVIOR

Introduction

Even though scientists have carried out thousands of experiments over the years in all disciplines of behavior, and discovered a lot of laws and elaborated many theories, there is still a need for one clear general explanation of phenomena associated with behavior.

So far a precise and effective definition of the following processes has not been reached: conditioning, learning, behavior, intelligence, problem solving and knowledge. Researchers had been satisfied with vague definitions and thus a restricted area could be attacked in order to discover less complex laws and to elaborate limited theories. Each school has developed a particular experimental method and a precise model which have often been successful. But then they tended to enlarge their system towards all other psychological phenomena, and were generally unsuccessful.

Only recently the interdisciplinary approach has become dominant. But there are many difficulties as far as methods, exchange of knowledge and integration of theories concerned, because each researcher substantially remains attached to his original principles. Now all the generic, redundant, incomplete and erroneous parts of each theory must be eliminated and the three sources of behavior (genetic, environmental and mental) have to be integrated into a wider organic framework.

The early behaviorists tended to be influenced by an obsessive sense of objectivity; and when faced with the subjects of their experiments they tended to lose the overall view of the phenomenon, in favor of the narrow aim of solving the problem at hand, that is the relationships S-S and R-S. Modern scientists of conditioning, who are fundamentally *connectionists* according to Hill (1990, p. 23), have changed their theories very much and have been moving towards a more cognitive and genetic perspective (e.g.,   Rescorla, 1988; Staddon, 1983).

However, up to now they have made use of Skinner's reasoning thus dividing conditioning in two types, classical and operant (see Mackintosh, 1983, chap. 2). This is an important point in that it blocks the process of integration.

Moreover, it is impossible to understand the mechanism of a complex information processor such as the brain only by defining some of its inputs and intervening variables. In spite of Hull's (1943) ingenious attempt, behaviorists did not really want to study behavior and could not do it, but ended up employing it to try to understand learning.

On the other hand some important studies, e.g., Breland and Breland's (1961) and Seligman's theory of preparedness (1970), have pointed out the importance of the genetic approach carried forward by *ethologists*. Also neurobiologists, from Bard onwards (the "sham rage", Bard, 1928), have confirmed that some behavior patterns are "stamped" in the brain. But ethologists have not produced a clear and well-structured formal analysis of behavior.

Now it is evident that some phenomena cannot be explained without looking inside the mind. Today the *cognitive* approach is prevalent in psychology. It has taken on a new lease on life since the mind has come to be considered a biological processor of information. The result of this is that an S-R analysis of behavior is no longer considered very relevant.

However all the complex structures and procedures that are programmed on computers, and which are necessary for human reason in order to understand events, often can be performed more simply and rapidly by any brain.

Finally in this perspective we enter into the mind but not into the brain, since, according to many computational cognitivists, hardware structures are not important, but rather the way programs are constructed (Johnson-Laird, 1983, pp. 9-10). Nevertheless, it is not easy to agree with this point, because it assumes that all the information processors, both biological and artificial, are substantially equivalent. On the other hand a detailed and comparative analysis of the anatomy of the brains of various species and hardware of computers of various types demonstrates that there are many differences between them that are reflected in their behavior and working. So we risk building models that work only in the researchers' minds and computers. Therefore the structures of all processors must be studied and, at the same time, correlated to their behavior mechanisms. Other researchers, however, have been working in this direction (e.g., see Kosslyn and Koenig, 1992, and their concept of "wet mind", pp. 3-4).

1) Classification

```
RELATION LIFE=BEHAVIOR
     PREPARATORY PHASE
          HABIT
                    GENETIC MEMORY
                    EPIGENETIC MEMORY
          ADAPTATION=PROBLEM SOLVING
                    NON-ORIGINAL SOLUTION
                         EXTERNAL
                                   IMITATION
                                   COMMUNICATION
                         INTERNAL
                                   GENETIC MEMORY
                                   EPIGENETIC MEMORY
                    ORIGINAL SOLUTION
                         EXTERNAL=LEARNING
                                   QUANTITATIVE
                                        HABITUATION
                                        SENSITIZATION
                                   ASSOCIATIVE
                                        CONDITIONING
                                        IMPRINTING
                         INTERNAL=INTELLIGENCE
     CONSUMMATORY PHASE
VEGETATIVE LIFE
```

Fig. 1 - Behavior process classification scheme.

The **relation life** or **behavior** (Fig. 1) is the relationship between the individual and his environment over time. The general purpose of behavior is to ensure the survival of the individual, his growth and his reproduction, in any given environmental condition. Thus he has some vegetative needs that he tries to satisfy. The relation life is made up of a series of parallel sensations and actions which are out of phase and which form "paths" (see sec. 2 - "The process model"). It is divided into two precise parts: the preparatory phase and the consummatory one.

The **preparatory phase** is characterized by the need to obtain an object that is necessary for the "endosoma" (see sec. 3 - "The structure model"), and that is satisfied by carrying out a pattern of behavior, e.g., fighting, courtship and predation, etc. In this phase there is a wide choice of paths, some of which are to be performed (rewarded) and others that should not be chosen (punished) in order to pass to the consummatory phase.

These behavior patterns can be modeled on the most recent habits, and thus derived from both *genetic memories* and *epigenetic* ones (see sec. 3 - "The structure model"). So in this case the preparatory phase is in the **habit** state.

Nevertheless over time some major and sudden mutations can occur in the environment or in the individual too. This new unpredictable situation invalidates the most recent habit behavior and brings the individual-environment relationship to a crisis. Thus a *problem* occurs, i.e. how to restore the right relationship with regard to satisfying a precise need. So the individual will look for a solution that is different from his most recent habits. This solution might have been used in the past, but not recently. Therefore we can say that the preparatory phase is in a state of **adaptation** (i.e. the present-day "problem solving" or "learning" in the wider sense), which is alternative to the habit state from which it is derived and towards which it tends. Its aim is to discover the path that leads to the consummatory phase, and when this path is stabilized, (i.e. often used in the same situations), it becomes a new habit. These solutions can be either original or non-original, in reference to the individual.

The *non-original solutions*, already existent, can be derived from outside the cerebrum, since it is connected to the environment, and this occurs either by **imitation** or by direct **communication**, or from inside by internal observation into *genetic* or *epigenetic memories*.

Otherwise, the individual can discover an *original solution* by himself, which may be totally new, at least for him. This also can come from two sources: inside or outside of the cerebrum.

The external solution occurs by way of trial and error in the real world. This is the mechanism of **learning**, a process in which the cerebrum establishes some strong associations between certain sensations and actions in the real world (cf. Mackintosh, 1983, p. 77; Mazur, 1990, p. 2). Experience is not the correct term to use here if the concept of knowledge is still linked to it, because this would cause us to be guilty of circular reasoning as described by Bower and Hilgard (1981, p. 2). The associations can be non-adaptive, or without any changes in behavior, or not resulting in performance: e.g., omission training of Coleman (1975), the blocked performance by atropine in Finch (1938), "latent learning" of Tolman (1932).

Here as well, the mechanism can be divided into two procedural modes: quantitative in which response modification either decreases (**habituation**) or increases (**sensitization**); and associative, where some new associations are formed among various elements, and is of two types, *conditioning* or *imprinting*.

The solutions elaborated inside the mind are the product of *intelligence*. In this mechanism the cerebrum elaborates many mental trials and later some of these "attempts" will be checked in the real world. Up to now this process has been called "thinking" or "problem solving" or "cognitive learning", but the use of these terms demonstrates lack of clarity in the classical definitions. For instance, Kohler in his paradigm with apes (1927, pp. 46-48) did not actually realize that he was not dealing just with learning, nor with a mere cognitive process, but with a mixture of several adaptive mechanisms. In fact ape Sultan, in the first part of the experiment, carries out some trials in the environment (learning state) which, after proving unsuccessful, he discontinues. In spite of this he goes on thinking about possible solutions until he foresees the right one in his mind and then this solution is performed by him immediately in the real world ("insight" phenomenon seen from outside).

When the individual discovers and obtains the object of need, then the *consummatory phase* is triggered. This phase is devoted to working on the object in the interface (see sec. 3 - "The structure model") between environment and endosoma, e.g., eating, copulation, urinating (cf. Von Bertanlaffy, 1950).

At the end of the activity in the consummatory phase the new object of need, if it has entered the soma, is further worked on as far as the individual's *vegetative life* is concerned. This occurs in parallel with the relation life and is completely automatic. It is made up of the main vegetative functions: digestion, reproduction, breathing, etc.; and in turn works on the objects up to the molecular level, which may be structural (e.g. proteins) or energetic (e.g. glucose). Moreover it has the function of internal micro-defense, e.g. with regard to bacteria.

Vice versa, if the object comes from the endosoma, and then is expelled during the consummatory phase, it is later free in the environment, concluding, in this way, the general cycle of the behavior process.

2) The process model

The process that puts into practice the above definitions has to be analyzed here (Fig. 2).

$$
\begin{bmatrix}
peS & \\
 & peA \\
--> & \\
 & piA \\
piS &
\end{bmatrix}_n
==>
\begin{bmatrix}
ceS & \\
 & ceA \\
--> & \\
 & ciA \\
ciS &
\end{bmatrix}_n
$$

Fig. 2 - Process model scheme.

```
(p = preparatory; c = consummatory;
 e = external; i = internal;
 S = Sensation; A = Action;
 n = ordinal number)
```

A **sensation** (*S*) is the representation in a certain moment of a sensorial field of the environment or of the soma in the cerebrum's input units (see sec. 3 - "The structure model"). The aim of every sensation is to prime a "good" subsequent action, and thus it is essentially a signal. Moreover every sensation causes either negative or positive feedback with regard to the previous action.

External sensation (*eS*) are sensations that refer to the environment. The individual has a series of eS that are made up of many elements that are difficult to know exactly. Hedonistically beautiful and ugly eS are defined by comparing them to others that are situated in the genetic and mass memories (cf. the "Innate releasing mechanism" used by ethologists, Lorenz, 1981, pp. 153-175). They are linked to a precise set of responses (piA and peA, see below) that marks each eS.

In the preparatory phase, an external Sensation (*peS*) is the survey of objects in the environment that can be either aversive or appetitive. The former stimulates an avoidance tendency and the latter, on the other hand, stimulate an approaching one. A peS can be a potential ceS (see below) or associated to another good or bad peS. During the preparatory phase the eS generally come from far ranging sensors: eyes, ears and nose.

In the consummatory phase, an external Sensation (*ceS*) is a gratifying sense of well-being regarding an object which is without doubt inside or outside of the soma. It can be either appetitive, i.e. the possession of the desired object (e.g. food) or aversive, i.e. the removal of an aversive one (e.g. shock, urine). In the consummatory phase eS usually comes from contact sensors: tongue, skin.

It should be pointed out that the object of a drive, which is sought by the "esosoma" (see sec. 3 - "The structure model"), might be different from the corresponding object of need that will be worked on by the endosoma. For example, a hungry baby will look for its mother's nipple, and the nipple is worked on during the consummatory phase, thus producing milk, which is the need of the endosoma and therefore of the vegetative life too.

An *internal sensation* (*iS*) is the representation of a soma's area, especially of the endosoma.

In the preparatory phase, the internal Sensation (*piS*) is a sense of inconvenience in the soma that can be either appetitive (e.g. hunger) or aversive (e.g. pain). It represents the individual's needs.

The individual associates certain piS (e.g. pain due to shock) with the corresponding peS (e.g. the shuttle-box) and he tends to react to the latter in order not to feel the corresponding piS.

During adaptation the parameters of the piS can change according to the situation. For example, a great increase in heart rate may occur after a shock because it is in support of a significant and immediate flight reaction. But if the adaptation has already occurred and if the solution does not imply doing heavy work, then the heart rate slows down in response to the same stimulus.

In the consummatory phase, the internal Sensations (*ciS*) are characterized by a gratifying sense from the endosoma that may be either appetitive (e.g., satiety, orgasm) or aversive (e.g., sense of well-being after pain). They terminate all the behavior patterns for that need.

An *action* (*A*) is a set of commands that at a certain moment the cerebrum's output units (see sec. 3 - "The structure model") give to the actuators which are, on the one hand, smooth muscles and glands, and, on the other, skeletal muscles. They can be contractions, relaxations and secretions, but all are integrated and coordinated. The goal is always to obtain a certain "interesting" sensation subsequently, and thus every action is of a selective and instrumental nature.

External actions (*eA*) are products of the skeletal muscles in response to the output units' commands which can come either from genetic memories or mass memories or may be partly new.

In the preparatory phase, external actions (*peA*) consist in setting a sensor and, if necessary, head and body, in one direction or manipulating an object. But each peA is both operant and perceptive at the same time. All peA are selective and their only aim is to reach the next interesting sensation (cf. Wickoff, 1952; Skinner, 1938). It is not important if this is reached by way of, for example, the hand muscles (e.g., adapting the fingers to a particular object's shape) or by the eye muscles. A peA can even be to remain motionless and to stare in a certain direction because the right sensation can only come from there. Moreover, even simply doing nothing can be very active and significant, e.g., a soldier who does not salute an officer!

In the consummatory phase, external actions (*ceA*) are those of the esosoma which work on the introduced object in the interface chambers in order to expel it from the soma, or to produce the substances directly usable by the endosoma (milk, sperm, bolus, etc.).

Internal actions (*iA*) are actions towards particular areas of the soma. They go along with the external ones, and often make the cerebrum aware of the endosoma's state. For instance, hypoglycemia becomes a *piA* (internal action in the preparatory phase) of hunger by way of stomach contractions. Moreover piA enable the soma to carry out the peA, e.g. all vegetative changes caused by fear which are in support of flight from unpleasant sensations.

In the consummatory phase, internal actions (ciA) follow rewards (ceS) but then, during adaptation, they can be anticipated in order to allow the beginning and the maintenance of the associated ceA: e.g., erection > copulation, salivation > chewing (cf. the atropinized dog that refuses food, Finch, 1938).

Actions are an integrated, complex and teleonomic set of responses of both the endosoma and the esosoma, and not simply tachycardia or salivation or lever pressing, as many conditioning theories have interpreted them. For example, flight is the peA of fear whose piA consists of tachycardia, shaking, etc. In Mowrer's "two-factor theory" (1947) the stimulus elicits the state of fear which in turn activates the skeletal response. Actually peA and piA occur at the same time; they are two aspects of one single response. However we can "feel fear" after carrying out the peA because some responses are slower to come about and to be noticed by the endosoma than others. For example, a man is driving calmly; suddenly he meets an obstacle on the road and applies the brakes firmly (peA), but only afterwards does he feel his heart beating very fast (piA > piS).

An important point is that in the case of indecisiveness two (or more) pA can be activated, bringing about a state of internal conflict (cf. Lorenz, 1981, pp. 243-245), in which one pA may try to produce an effect and the other pA an effect completely opposite at the same time.

The *preparatory phase* is characterized by the discovery and the obtaining of the object to be worked on or by creating the conditions for the priming of the consummatory phase. The preparatory phase: (1) can be either appetitive or aversive; (2) allows the adaptation to take place even though it may be formed by some genetic chunks; and in addition, (3) it is very highly developed in humans as well as being complex and indirect with respect to the consummatory phase.

The law of adaptation involves always starting with a punishment, which can be either "appetitive omissive" (e.g. lack of food) or "aversive effective" (e.g. shock), and terminating with the last reward. Reward can be either "appetitive effective" (e.g. possessing food) or "aversive omissive" (e.g. absence of shock). This definition is clearer than Skinner's (1953, p. 73) because the terms "reinforcement" and "reinforcer", along with their positive and negative modifiers, are sometimes confusing since they have been used with various meanings.

Some examples of the preparatory phase are the behavior patterns of hunting and courtship, which, in the consummatory phase, are followed by eating and copulation respectively. Pecking and biting are not the initial action of the consummatory phase but rather the last one of the preparatory one.

In some cases the preparatory phase may not be followed by the corresponding consummatory one. For example, in the behavior patterns concerning play and exploration the individual has not got a vegetative need but, nevertheless, searches in the same way without activating the ceA. Another example of this phenomenon is when an individual is hunting, and this is not followed by eating or, in the case of courtship, mounting which is not followed by copulation (cf. Lorenz, 1981, pp. 325-335). This is a good example how different mechanisms (e.g., genetics, imitation and learning) can converge to obtain the correct behavior. For example, in rhesus monkeys the mounting by the male over the female's posterior legs, which is the last part of the preparatory phase, must be acquired during its early social life by observation and play. In fact, males reared in isolation are neither capable of doing this adequately nor of copulation (Harlow, 1962).

The *consummatory phase* is the interface period between environment and endosoma. It is distinguishable in that it: (1) consists of actions which precede those of the endosoma and are coordinated with them; (2) occurs in the interface chambers; (3) has paths which are standard and genetic; (4) can be inactive (e.g., rest or sleep), or active introductive (e.g., food, water, sperm), or active expulsive (e.g., feces, urine, fetus); (5) is the second and final phase of relation life, that terminates a particular behavior, thus satisfying a certain need.

In humans the consummatory phase assumes some complex characteristics derived from civilization (e.g., feasts), and although it is more separated from important preparatory behavior patterns that really are of support to it, it is always present in everyday life. For example, civilized man finds it is easy to get food, the difficult thing is to make money in order to acquire it!

This phase as well can run independently without a need or other drives: e.g., a small monkey sucking a breast without milk, the "rage copulation", etc.

The above definitions regarding the preparatory and consummatory phases are different from other ones, for instance the nebulous one of Konorski (1967), the one more precise of Woodworth (1958, p. 223) and the most important one of ethologists (Craig, 1918). This last definition states that motivation leads the individual to be in a state of continuous agitation, that is "appetitive" or "searching" or "preparatory" behavior. For example, a hungry eagle apparently flies aimlessly over a valley until it meets a "key stimulus" (e.g. a rabbit) which triggers the consummatory act, i.e. attacking, capturing and eating. Whereas, according to the model presented here, the consummatory phase begins only when the food is in its mouth without the possibility of being threatened and thus lost (ceS). From this perspective all the stages concerning the sighting of potential reward and its actual capture can be either in a state of adaptation or in one of habit, e.g., a lion may have learned that zebras are always near a river...

The **behavioral path** is a series of cycles of sensation and action. In the adaptation state the right path must be discovered that leads to the ceS, thus solving the problem. This occurs by producing and selecting various S-A cycles that seem to be correct. Some of them can then be eliminated because they are recognized as being superfluous, even if they were useful at the beginning in order to reach the goal. Chunks of some paths can be copied, divided, modified, erased or even linked to form a new path.

During the adaptation state the individual records in his mass memory a lot of paths that are not all right or useful for that action. But in the future he may refer back to them using these associations for different situations. This phenomenon is called "latent learning" (Tolman, 1932), but this is not the right term for it. In fact, the association is latent but the mechanism that brought it about is always evident.

The paths of the preparatory phase are a mixture derived from different sources: conditioning, intelligence, genetic memory and epigenetic memory...

Sometimes it is impossible for an individual to solve the problem or it is difficult to discriminate the most correct path from those available, and so some paradoxical, strange or negative phenomena may occur: autoshaping, partial reinforcement effect, omission training, learned helplessness and superstition, etc.

Moreover, many potential paths inscribe themselves on a behavioral network of possible events which can be analyzed by using a cognitive approach.

3) The structure model

Now we must describe the major elements presented in the following diagram regarding the individual, the brain and the mind, as a support of the general mechanisms expressed above (Fig. 3).

ENVIRONMENT

```
              :
          ESOSOMA
              :
      ┌──────────────────┐  a
  s   │        :         │  c
  e   │    CEREBRUM      │  t
  n   │        :         │  u
  s   ├──────────────────┤  a
  o   │        :         │  t
  r   │    ENDOSOMA      │  o
      │        :         │  r
      └────┬─────────┬───┘
           │    :    │
           │ i : c   │
           │    :    │
```

Fig. 3 - Structure model diagram.

(ic = interface chamber)

Every highly structured biological being, i.e. humans and superior species of animals, can be divided into two fundamental parts: the *cerebrum*, i.e. the brain plus spinal cord normally known as the central nervous system, and the *soma*, i.e. the rest of the body. The soma in turn is divided into two parts: the *esosoma*, i.e. muscles and bones, that regards the relation life; and the *endosoma*, i.e. viscera, that concerns the vegetative life. They work in parallel and are complementary and coordinated each other. Both the esosoma and the endosoma have an input section made up of *sensors* (molecules, cells, organs such as eyes) and an output one, consisting of *actuators* (muscle fibers, muscles, glands). The soma is the sensory-mechanical apparatus of the individual and the cerebrum is his information processor, which checks and commands all of the soma's elements. The cerebrum is in contact with the environment by way of the esosoma.

The *interface chambers*, which are a bridge between the endosoma and the environment, are the channels of the soma at the boundary of the eso- and endosoma: mouth, vagina, nipple-ducts, rectum, etc. Normally they are closed but can extend themselves even very much in the presence of an object that must be worked on during the consummatory phase (e.g. penis, fetus, nipple, bolus, urine, feces). They often have smooth and skeletal muscles whose actions are coordinated in order to work on and introduce or expel objects.

The cerebrum has a structure that is made up of: (1) external input units, (2) internal input units, (3) external output units, (4) internal output units, (5) processing units; (6) genetic sensor memory units, (7) genetic actuator memory units, (8) epigenetic sensor memory units, and (9) epigenetic actuator memory units.

The cerebrum elaborates (processes) two types of information: sensations and actions, and so it has a sensorial section and an actuative one. The information patterns are elaborated independently and in parallel. This does not mean that in order to have a correct analysis of behavior the out of phase scheme (Fig. 4) must not be used.

```
    ... eS1 --> eS2 --> eS3 --> eS4   ...

      ... eA1 --> eA2 --> eA3 --> eA4   ...

      ... iA1 --> iA2 --> iA3 --> iA4   ...

    ... iS1 --> iS2 --> iS3 --> iS4   ...
```

Fig. 4. Cerebrum activity scheme.

```
(e = external;  i = internal;
 S =  Sensation;  A = Action)
```

During sensation each input unit, already connected to the soma's sensor and thus to the environment or endosoma, is in turn connected to the memory. During action the same thing happens with other memories and output units, that in turn are connected to their corresponding actuators of the esosoma which act in the environment, or to those of the endosoma.

The recording and the maintenance of all sensations and actions and their paths, the wrong ones as well, take place in various memories. The genetic memories of behavior are ROM-like (read only memory) and are common to all individuals of that species and change only by genetic mutation. The epigenetic memories are mass memory-like and record the individual's experience and change continuously.

During learning the memory units are in contact with the environment and the soma through the input and the output units. Whereas during the mechanism of intelligence a part of the cerebrum is not in contact with the outside (i.e. the soma and the environment). Indeed the processing units exchange information between the memory units and the input units (or a hypothetical working memory). In this way the cerebrum can simulate reality and all its possible manipulations without moving matter and without energy consumption (cf. Kosslyn, 1983). Then the hypothetical correct action or path will be transferred to and verified in the real world by the esosoma.

III. EMOTIONS-FEELINGS: AGAIN, WHAT ARE THEY? AND HOW MANY ARE THERE?

Introduction

Although it is now clear that most of the exact aspects of emotions have already been identified in one theory or another, the questions posed in the title still apply today. One has the impression of going round the problem in circles but still without grasping the structure of the process and, therefore, without having an overall picture. The great theories of the past tackled the issue from physiological expressions (e.g. Schachter and Singer, 1962), from facial expressions (e.g. Ekman, 1982), with linguistic analyses (e.g. Johnson-Laird and Oatley, 1989) and then with meticulous analysis of appraisal after cognitivism became domineering (e.g. Schorr, 2001). Lastly, and rightly so, we are now turning increasingly towards research in the neurosciences in order to identify the structures of the brain that produce these phenomena (e.g. Panksepp, 1998; Davidson, Scherer and Goldsmith, 2003). The need remains, however, for a correct guiding criterion in order to understand precisely what emotions are, so as to know exactly which are and which are not emotions, and to define the middle level between the upper phenomenological-behavioral one and the lower neurobiological one in approaching these studies (cf. Frijda, 2004, p. 171). The aim of this paper is precisely to focus on the problems preventing the solution from being reached and to provide a consequential, original and complete solution.

These problems are:

1) Emotion is a behavior and without a valid behavioral theory behind it, it is impossible to have a valid theory on emotion. This work is based on a definite theory of behavior that I exposed in the previous chapter.

2) There has always been confusion among needs, motivations, feelings and emotions, "emotional response", "bodily response", etc. Such words as love, disgust, good /bad, positive and negative, and many others are used in a very ambiguous way not only in everyday life but also in the scientific literature. As is the case in natural sciences (for example, the concept of *force*), it is now unavoidable to clarify these definitions precisely and synthetically.

3) Lastly, although emotions are "pre-packaged" actions, they try to respond to a logic of adaptation on the part of the individual, and can, therefore, be analysed functionally on the basis of three precise axes of interpretation, that we shall examine later.

1) What is an emotion?

First of all, we must mention the still present century-old controversy between James and Cannon (James, 1884; Cannon, 1929), in which these authors unwittingly posed a fundamental question that is not among those normally considered, that is to say: are emotions basically sensations or actions? (cf. Izard, 1990; Scherer, 2000, pp. 154-156)

Before James, the first traditional and common sense theories considered emotions above all as sensations, followed by a response. As we can interpret and express, these sensations were visceral states and the responses to them were voluntary acts: I see a bear > "I am scared" > I run away (see Fig. 5).

Afterwards, James continuing along the same basic line, became fully conscious that emotions in this outlook are sensations, but: "emotions are embodied, that they emanate from the physical self and not from some 'spiritual' source outside a person's experience of self" as in the folk version (Barbalet, 2004, p. 221). Then he observed that these sensations must be the result of an "act", and very simply – but causing quite a clamor - reversed the process (combining, among other things, autonomic responses with skeletal responses): I see the bear > I tremble /I run away (note that these two types of responses were not together in paradigms he did) > I am scared.

In spite of this, his paradox was exactly here: the voluntary response came before the emotional sensation and, therefore, in order to escape criticism he willingly minimized it in some passages (cf. Ellsworth, 1994, p. 225, about the James' replay to Dr. Worchester's objection). For this reason, in recent decades the new cognitivists have substantially split up the response into an autonomic response, followed by the sensation-emotion, that is the feeling, and a voluntary response, preceded by a second appraisal (cf. Lazarus, 1991). In this way, moreover, the second and unappreciated aspect of these theories is highlighted, that is to say, either the total separation of the autonomic responses and the skeletal ones (cognitivists), or their merger without maintaining their diversity (James).

Cannon, on the other hand, was the unconscious but firm upholder of a radically different concept, that emotions are essentially actions, although no great distinction was made between external voluntary actions and autonomic ones.

THEORIES	PHASES					
Folks	Perception			"Emotion"		Skeletal R
James	Perception		Autonomic R or Skeletal R	"Emotion"		
Cognitivists	Perception	Appraisal 1 (Emotion)	Autonomic R (Emotion)	Feeling (Emotion)	Appraisal 2 (Emotion)	Skeletal R (Emotion)
Cannon	Perception			Autonomic R + Skeletal R		

Fig. 5 - Scheme of emotions' phases. (R = response)

Thus, according this line but in a new framework, an *emotion* is a simple, archaic and genetic set of integrated and purposeful movements and secretions, that is inscribed in the ROM MEMORIES. That is they are pre-made actions! That is they are compound of *internal Action* and *external Action* (see chap. II, sec. 2 - "The process model"). Running away is the fear! Notwithstanding, these actions often cannot be implemented in full.

They are *superior instincts*, that is, behaviors, stereotyped motor programs from the Preparatory Phase, at least in superior mammals, while we consider the functions of the Consummatory Phase (breathing, eating, etc.) *inferior instincts*.

A *feeling* is nothing more than a lighter emotion, that is not transformed immediately into direct, strong action but does have an important influence on reasoning and facial expression. Thus, the sensory aspect is secondary, not as the word would have us believe! It is the other name for emotions, an important but misleading aspect that struck researchers working along James' line. More than anything else it is a *motion*, "a tendency to...". The more an individual is calm and reflective, the more easily he will adopt complex and structured actions. These actions can also be ***intelligent***, even if there is always a certain underlying predominant feeling towards a given situation, that limits and conditions the unconscious production of certain solutions rather than others, in the logical direction imposed by feeling.

Like all targeted actions, emotion obviously has an aspect towards the body (the *internal Action)* and one towards the environment (the *external Action*) which are integrated, parallel and synergic one to the other. That is to say, one automatic and within the body and one voluntary and external to it, that induces the body to move and to manipulate the environment. It is clear, therefore, that James was also right in a way: if all the expressions of an emotion, e.g. of fear, are eliminated, that emotion disappears. But we must be careful: fear means running away, but often we do not want to do it immediately, and while the internal Action is activated directly (heartbeat, tightness of the stomach, etc., but also the use of the skeletal body leading to increased muscle tone and specific postures and facial expressions), the external Action is presented to the Voluntary Decision-making System, which decides whether to implement it or not, or which chooses another emotion or a motion produced cognitively by thought. Indeed, at this level there are *motions*, that is to say, proposals of external Actions of cognitive or emotional origin. For this reason, there may also be contemporary and opposite activations in the soma, and therefore the occurrence of a state of internal conflict that generates stress. It is like driving a car, accelerating while the brake is on: the car does not move, but the effort is imposing.

If, on the other hand, the feeling becomes very strong (that is an emotion arises in the classic sense with an escalation), this motion will have such force that takes over the individual completely, and will be put into practice immediately and with decision, including its external Action part.

Over the millennia, evolution has selected these actions in the life of mammals and of man in particular, for the purpose of objectifying need, adapting it to a particular situation. If I do not choose something, how can I sooner or later satisfy my need? The brain detects the molecular and energy or defensive deficits, that is the *needs* of the body, by means of certain more or less clear and specific *internal Sensations*, that, therefore, become *motivations*. But then, through the esosoma, it must choose, find and conquer the specific objects that can potentially satisfy these needs. Thus, in the case of hunger, this means having a specific food. Lions do not eat grass but meat, in the form of a zebra, for example. But which zebra, and where and when? Without this automatic process – except for today's scientifically super-evolved human species – how does one know what to eat, where it is and how to obtain it?

The after-Sensations (internal Sensations of feelings) that record automatic activations following an internal Action are epiphenomena of emotions (e.g. the internal Sensation of tachycardia) that, however, also serve to make the individual aware of his emotional state, and to press him to act in a way that will enable him to reduce tension.

The Sensory Emotional Circuits evaluate the environmental Stimulus, the *external Sensations*, comparing them with genetic *external Sensation patterns* stored in the ROM MEMORIES or with earlier similar external Sensations and thoughts also stored in MASS MEMORIES. If they are found to correspond, the Actuative Emotional Circuits that produce the emotion action are activated automatically, unconsciously and directly. All these processes take place in parallel and are, of course, constantly up-dated and influence one another.

Within this framework, therefore, it is logical to interpret *mood* as the prevailing feeling over a certain period of time and *passion* as a very strong feeling with respect to an object or a very precise aim, that may even last for a long time (many years) and is perhaps reinforced, from time to time, by various suitable emotions.

2) How many emotions are there?

At this point we can say that if emotions are well targeted and integrated movements, they are of a well-defined number and have definite functions (for the debate on basic emotions see, e.g., Sabini and Silver, 2005; Solomon, 2002). For this reason, there must be some logical axes for interpreting them that define them rationally. In my opinion, these can be clearly identified by means of functional analysis. They are: "beautiful" /"ugly", superior /inferior, "pre" /"post", that is to say: aesthetics, power ratio, verification.

The **aesthetic** point of view is the first feature of an object or a situation. It is the recognition that a given thing is significant for a certain need, on the basis of specific characteristics. Obviously, there is the usual directionality: keeping something beautiful /escaping something ugly, getting rid of something ugly /looking for something beautiful. The distinction between having something ugly (e.g., pain) and not having something beautiful (e.g., not obtaining food) is purely formal and linguistic. A feeling (e.g., an ugly feeling) remains, that differs only in terms of intensity and urgency, but in the long term it is always very negative (pain is more urgent but also unsatisfied hunger will lead to death!). We should not confuse internal Sensations (pain /hunger) with the external Sensations with which they are associated (e.g., fire /food), whether present or absent.

Then the perceived **power ratio** between the individual and the "other" (person, animal, object, circumstances, groups, god, etc.) is essential for determining whether I can have something that, although it is beautiful, might not be achievable (as we all know very well). So what is the point of making an effort? The more this ratio is unbalanced the clearer is the emotion, the more this ratio is balanced the more two conflicting emotions are rising.

Finally, a *critical event* is an effort, a struggle that can decide the win or the loss in a certain affair, often without reaching the extreme consequences (e.g., the threat that forces somebody to flee). The main function of a **POST-critical event** emotion is to sanction a possible change in a PRE-emotion associated with a specific Stimulus. Indeed, the post-emotions occur after a significant event, and do not contribute towards its occurrence. So what is their purpose? Do they function merely as a release? (cf. Frijda, 1994). For example, if, having come across a specific object such as something that has attacked me and caused me to run away many times, this time I fight and win (critical event), then this will make me happy and the emotion associated with it in the future will no longer be fear but aggressiveness. These emotions are, indeed, often characterized by surprise, and the more the event becomes customary the less strong the emotions will be. Further proof is provided by the fact that in all PRE-feelings one looks towards and thinks of the future, while with POST-feelings one looks back at and thinks of the past, of the fact that has occurred. In addition, obviously, they mark the object in question positively or negatively in an aesthetic sense.

PRE-emotions have also been called *drives, motivations, expectations,* while POST-emotions have been called *gratification* and *frustration*. It should be stressed, on the other hand, that *punishment /negative reinforcement, reward /positive reinforcement* are external Sensations, not actions.

		PRE-	POST-	
Ugly	inferior	**Fear**	**Disappointment**	ugly-inferior
	superior	**Aggressiveness**		
Beautiful	inferior	**Desire**	**Happiness**	beautiful-superior
	superior	**Love**		

Fig. 6 – Synoptic table of emotions and their axes of interpretation.

There are four PRE-emotions: fear, aggressiveness, love and desire.

In *fear* (that is to say *anxiety, anguish, panic, terror,* clearly in order of intensity and escalation), something ugly has or is about to come along: I am inferior and I can avoid it. Fear is escaping, flight in an open field (= external Action, the internal Action is evident: tachycardia, trembling, etc.). A far-off external Sensation that recalls a frustrating one will be quickly escaped from. In *anxiety* the negative external Sensation may not be very obvious, but on analyzing it carefully it can always be found, except in the case of strictly pathological anxiety that is disconnected from appropriate and proportional Stimuli.

Aggressiveness (that is to say *irritation, antipathy, contempt, hate, anger, rage, ferocity, fury*): something ugly has or is about to come along but I am superior, so I threaten, attack, fight and destroy it. The same applies to somebody or something preventing me from obtaining the beautiful thing I want, for example food (cf. Berkowitz and Harmon-Jones, 2004). In social contexts there is also a communicative aspect: he should not have taken the liberty of doing that within the group in which I dominate!

Love is the feeling of giving something beautiful or of getting rid of something ugly. It is probably substantiated in the Parental Instinct Circuit. All the adjectives used unconsciously in situations of that kind recall that relationship. I am superior and will be happy when I have given something beautiful. It is often the fruit of joy. The corresponding emotions are smiling, caressing, hugging, giving. It is understood here as a basic emotion. Romantic love is a complex emotion (that is a mixture of love, desire and joy, with often some ugly ones) the object of which is sexuality;

not to mention Christian love that also has other fundamental connotations such as ethical and metaphysical ones (cf. Djikic and Oatley, 2004).

Desire (*search, hope, interest*), on the other hand, is wanting to receive beautiful things that I do not have since I am inferior. It means approaching with anticipation, wagging one's tail and imploring. It is seeking, working to obtain something (cf. Silvia, 2005).

There are only two POST-emotions: happiness and disappointment.

Happiness or *joy* is when an individual has won and a PRE- feeling has been satisfied, no matter whether it is by having or giving or destroying or escaping! It up-dates the positive mark of that external Sensation as a possible and good object of consummation. This emotion is expressed in the form of skipping, laughter, specific mimicry, dancing, feasting, etc.

At this point, we have to make a note about "positive" emotions. They were ignored in all the old models of theories, because they are very evasive and nebulous without a solid framework of interpretation when analyzed. In fact, only recently have they been taken in consideration, not regarding their meaning, but rather for their capability of adaptation, that is, for their appropriateness and moral judgment (see, e.g., Fredrickson, 2004; Solomon and Stone, 2002; Ben-Ze'ev, 2000).

In **disappointment** (or *moral suffering, sorrow, sadness, melancholy, depression, desperation*), something ugly has come or is coming, but one is too inferior and is unable to escape it: *les jeux sont faits...* In its physiological form it serves the purpose of disinvesting our desire from an object that is no longer beautiful and /or that cannot be obtained, enabling us to pass to other ways of meeting a need. When it is very strong, it concerns life itself and serious depression sets in, leading to abandoning oneself to death (in animals) or to even actively seeking it (in man). Man blames himself morally for the fact. He keeps thinking of the past, of the ugly fact: post-emotions. He moves away from the object, and for some time solitude is sought. He is weak, submissive and withdrawn; he cries, etc.

It is clear that physical *pain* is a Sensation, a different one from those that occur in fear and in depression (or moral pain, although they are often associated), and this has also been demonstrated by experimental data as far back as the time of lobotomy, which eliminated the emotional aspect while maintaining the sensory aspect which was no longer disturbing (cf. Damasio, 1999, chap 2.). Furthermore, pain can be easily associated with anger! It is an internal Sensation not only of the visceral body but also of the sensors that are found throughout the body, except for the brain, of course.

Surprise (*startle, wonder*) are not emotions but a sudden change from one emotion to another, in reference to Sensations the second of which (in order of time) is unexpected in relation to the first (e.g., desire > fear, I open a box thinking there is a beautiful clothes whereas I find a snake!), and so this change may be either beautiful or ugly. Similarly, *disgust* is not an emotion but, as in the original Latin meaning, a non-emotional action expressed mainly facially, a lower instinct opposite to that of eating (and then swallowing), as a reaction to an ugly external Sensation of taste (and then vomiting). When it is understood as being *moral repugnance* or *contempt*, it is a sort of aggressiveness (cf. Royzman and Sabini, 2001).

Frustration, envy and *jealousy* are often a complex situation, made up of more than one feeling of inconvenience (depression, anger, fear) that alternate and stimulate each other.

It is also possible to detect emotions in man due to cognitive reasons that we could call meta-emotions, e.g. *irony*, when something absurd occurs or is hypothesized (e.g., I laugh seeing a mouse threatening to beat up a lion in a cartoon), or social emotions of fear, such as *shyness*, or of aggression, such as *derision*.

Doubt as to whether something is negative is not due to fear but to a *conflict* between two or more feelings. It is possible to have more than one feeling towards an object at the same time, and they may be conflicting! What is more, an emotion easily spreads to objects that have nothing to do with it or even to what could be useful. The action is discharged onto someone else, like a person who ruins his home rather than facing his enemy, or takes it out on his wife... since these are inferior. Or an emotion referred to a more important *behavioral path* becomes another emotion in an inferior *cycle* (see chap. II, sec. 2 - "The process model"). For example, if I am scared of arriving late at an important meeting with my boss, I get angry with the little old woman driving the car in front of me who will not let me overtake her! Lastly, PATHOLOGICAL feelings are the result of dissonance between the objective problem and the way in which the emotional person perceives it, which is often completely distorted. For others, the Emotional Circuits may also be hypertonic and /or completely illogically disconnected from the corresponding Stimuli (e.g., a person who laughs at a funeral).

IV. THE CONCEPTS OF *LOVE* FROM THE NEUROSCIENCE POINT OF VIEW

Introduction

Among the various languages and cultures, never have we encountered more discrepancies than those found in the concepts of happiness, love and good. Love is one of the most used and important words of our everyday life and is greatly employed in the arts (especially music and literature) as well as in religions and now also in human sciences. However, its basic concepts are very complicated, blurred and confused. This word is currently utilized also in neurosciences and this requires a clear definition of its different meanings. This will result in a contribution to the other disciplines that use this term.

Several classifications have been attempted in psychology, such as Sternberg's Triangular Theory that is rather confused (Sternberg, 1986, important for its third axis "commitment"), but also that of Berscheid (2010) is limited, although clearer and logically structured.

Philosophers have never completely defined what love really is, a topic as elusive as apparently intuitive. They have investigated love as passion, looking for its consequences, not its deep meaning, or only in a metaphorical valence of metaphysics and gnoseology, that is impressive but vague.

Herein I try to identify and define all its main meanings, in the light of my integrated Theory of Behavior and that of Emotions. As we shall understand at the end, it is essential to determine the fundamental ones without duplications or mixtures deriving from different languages, cultures or theoretical models, without leaving out even one of them, as they are all profoundly, structurally and procedurally interwoven.

Basic concepts

1) Love as a *pleasant sensation*

First of all, we should focus on a very important, misunderstood and elusive meaning, which is however clear according to my theoretical system, that is love as a sensation. In various languages, but above all in French, the word love has a meaning that can be compared to the verb *to like:* for instance, *je aime la marmelade* ("I like /love marmalade"). However, this is a process that regards the cerebral analysis of sensations. Therefore, for every sense of the body there is a pleasure, not only for taste (e.g., a "good" food commonly said), for smell (a "good" smell, a perfume), for touch (pleasure when touching a certain surface), but also for hearing (harmony of a sound, music, a voice) and for sight (a landscape, a figure, a painting, a beautiful face).

In synthesis, these sensations automatically, instantaneously and unconsciously receive a beautiful or ugly connotation as soon as they arise, that is the stimulus is felt.

Furthermore, as already seen in the Theory of Emotions, I attribute the adjective *beautiful* not only to all pleasant sensation but also to every type of pleasant emotion.

It is obvious that one attempts to possess "beautiful" things (and shuns "ugly" things), but not always. This falls within the fundamental law of our nature and the concept of beautiful, that is its desirableness. However, this substantiates a different type of love, even if it is closely linked to it according to aesthetic logics, as we shall see in the following section.

2) Love as a basic feeling: *desire*

In this situation, an individual thinks of one thing, looks for it, moves and fights to have it. He is in the Preparatory Phase of behavior. It is a fundamental feeling-emotion that we have identified in the Theory of Emotions (chap. III).

Filial love is its prototype. It is a drive to have protection and help by the small child from the big parent. The brain circuits are most likely these (cf. Bowlby's *attachment behavior theory*, 1969). As one grows older, it expands and is applied to all the situations in which one is inferior and seeks something.

Eros as a "vital impulse" (cf. Plato, 400 BC c.; Freud, 1920) might be substantially attributed to desire according to this meaning, that is the drive to have, do, achieve, possess, attain, construct and evolve. Without it one could not live, nothing would change. Paradoxically, in certain undertakings and conceptions, not to risk failure (especially when meeting others), one even tries to completely eliminate it (cf. Schopenauer, 1819).

The application of desire to sexual needs leads to seeking a partner and in this concrete case it is called *eros* in Greek; sexual desire is the most precise and clearest definition of this word.

This meaning should be differentiated from that of *pleasure* in the previous section. I would like to point out that also in English *to like* means to be pleased by and to desire. My theories make the subtle but unequivocal distinction clear between love as a pleasant sensation and as an emotion-desire because, logically, I desire what is pleasant, beautiful, and what is beautiful is often desirable too. However this is not always the case: I can be in the phase of satiation or unable to reach it (the fox and the grapes, for instance), or subjectively dislike it. Sure enough they are two totally different functions: the first one is a sensation, the second an action (cf. Sternberg, 1987).

Furthermore, in this regard, a great imbalance leads to a type of "selfish love": thinking only of ourselves, in an obsessive and exasperated but vain search for newer and greater objects and positions to posses, with the illusion of finding happiness in them. Therefore, all this may lead (but not always) to desperation and apathy.

Finally, this meaning is often understood as being the only one for love, which is one of the aspects that brings about more misunderstandings in the human soul and behavior, especially in relationships of couples. Therefore, it requires a clear differentiation also from the subsequent, symmetrical and opposite meaning, with which it might be sometimes in conflict.

3) Love as a basic feeling: *love*

This concept is love as a basic feeling in my sense of the word according to the Theory of Emotion (see chap. III); it is to have the beautiful and giving it to another. It is the most profound and fullest meaning of the word love. For this reason, I chose it as the name of this fundamental feeling-emotion, at least in the sphere of neurosciences. It is an emotional action and here too we are in the Preparatory Phase of behavior. It is altruistic love that does not expect any response (Dessler, 1930 c.).

It is probably based on parental behavior, parents' love for their children, as we stated in chapter III, and in this regard see the theories of *caregiving behavior* (Bowlby, 1969) and *compassionate love* (Fehr et al., 2009).

The extension of this concept to the METAPHYSICAL and THEOLOGICAL aspect in Christianity has been of great importance throughout history, but at the theoretical level it has overshadowed the moral one as we shall see shortly. Indeed, in Christian terminology *agape* is another name that can be better considered as a synonym for it. However, at this point agape proves to be a composite and ambiguous term as it also certainly integrates the other element that we shall see in section 5.

Furthermore, it should be pointed out that also this kind of love can lead to psychological and moral errors when it is excessive and misdirected.

4) Love as *sexuality*

One of the most common and evident meanings is love in the sexual sense. It substantially corresponds to the Consummatory Phase of sexual instinct that is to mating, "having sex" in the crudest expression currently predominant in western culture. It is the final part of *erotic love in the strictest sense*.

Nowadays there are well-defined specific brain circuits for this purpose.

Indeed, at this point, *eros* proves to be a complex and ambiguous concept consisting of love as a desire for a sexual object and love as sex practiced.

As outlined in the chapter II on behavior, the process of sexuality, separated from other psychological, social and ethical aspects, implies a *sexual need,* a search for (a desire of a sexual type, see sec. 2, this chapter) and a meeting with a potentially satisfying partner (a suitable beautiful as in sec. 1, this chapter), the struggle to conquer and possess him /her. At this point, the Consummatory Phase is triggered and, in this case, it consists of sexual intercourse.

However, as previously mentioned, also here its biological meaning is often surpassed to obtain a wider one: in Italian the expression "to make love" was also used, that is to stay with one's fiancé in an ambiguously romantic sense with the creation of a family in view. Even more generally, such a profound union of bodies, the "suspension" of conscience and the "ecstasy" of orgasm have also suggested a METAPHYSICAL conception starting from sexuality. The Bible says "they know each other" and "will be one flesh", and will actually bear a new human being. Even more, there have been communities whose religion has seen in this a means of *union* with the divinity: see sacred prostitution.

5) Love as a *moral* concept

In sections 2, 3 and 4, I did not develop new elements but amply clarified the concepts of love to be connected with analogous definitions of the integrated Theory of Behavior and that of Emotions of the previous chapters. Now it is necessary to single out a key aspect that has been scarcely identified and that is clearly of a different nature, i.e. philosophical, because all these theories are based on it. That's why, so far, I have always spoken of "beautiful" and "ugly", because "good" and "evil" fall within another category. Indeed, a careful analysis reveals that love has an additional aspect besides the biological and psychological-social ones, that is the philosophical-religious one, that is real, is part of everyday life and with which one must theoretically confront oneself also to link it with the others. *Over the centuries and in different cultures this concept has been inadvertently mixed and confused with the others.*

In spite of the fact that in the philosophical sphere several concepts of love may be partly linked with those previously described and clearly referred to neurosciences (for instance, *eros* can be shifted from supernatural movement to desire and its power and, therefore, to the possession of things and even knowledge, as in Plato), we can undoubtedly identify some precise METAPHYSICAL concepts of love, such as, for example, the unifying energy of Empedocles (460 BC c.), that of the Romantics as a relationship between the finite and the infinite, or even that of Christianity according to which God *is* love (the Holy Bible, 1 Jn. 4.8, a very strange and revolutionary definition in comparison with the gods *of* love of Greco-Roman antiquity).

Above all, in this section, we must stress the existence of the **concept of love as a requirement and a moral precept,** that is

love = *doing good.*

On the other hand, to say "I love you" the Italians often say: *Ti voglio bene* ("I want good for you" literally translated). In this short and simple but important phrase there is certainly an aesthetic aspect but, in particular, it expresses a moral aspect in a powerful way. Is love only a game or a psychic or sexual technique? Love as a pure feeling is evidently spontaneous and difficult to control; love that has a moral aspect is exercised by the will according to acquired schemes of values, most likely structured on determined ethics and cultures.

But, what is love in the more specific moral sense, synthesized into doing good? For now, in my opinion we can say that it means profoundly considering our humanity also in others and, therefore, respect them and help them concretely.

Love as a moral value regards the contents of one's actions. For instance, in the gustatory sense, "good" food (i.e. *beautiful* according to my definition) is often *good* also in the moral sense (good with regard to nutrition of the body) and, therefore, to be sought and obtained. By contrast, unrestrained desires are a clear example of the opposite meaning. For example, I want to change cars, I would really like a spider, but I have three children and I cannot afford two cars: my affectivity directs me towards a spider but my moral sense forces me to buy a station wagon.

At this point, the following meanings should be specified:

- by *aesthetics* I intend not so much the study of artistic representation, but rather our sensitivity and affectivity that continuously analyze the environment in the exterior sense and to which they react automatically and instantaneously. That is, it concerns the beautiful = pleasant and the ugly = disagreeable, real, as found by the individual;

- *ethics* or *morality*: human behavior and its analysis, in relation to the substance of things, to the content of entities (objects, persons and actions), rationally evaluating them as good ("good" ones) or evil ("bad" ones), that is to be pursued or shunned.

However, it should be stressed that the beautiful, as intended herein, means any pleasant sensation or emotion, not only that of sight or hearing, but also of taste (a food commonly said "good") and of touch, e.g. receiving a caress. And also a mathematician who solves a complicated problem will have "rational pleasure", that is nothing else than the happiness of having solved a problem, perhaps combined with the visual and audible pleasure of a formally elegant solution (many mathematicians unconsciously express themselves in this aestheticizing way). "Biological evil" is pain in an aesthetical way, is a sensation (which is often linked with ugly emotions and, possibly, to moral evil). Thus, beautiful emotions (desire, love and happiness in particular) fall within the sphere of aesthetics, they too are "the beautiful" (and, by contrast, ugly emotions are "the ugly": fear, rage, and delusion).

The concept of *agape* in the Christian sense falls decidedly within this context, even if it is now clear that this is a complex and ambiguous concept, in which there is love as feeling-love (sec. 3) and love as a moral concept (this section). For this reason, it does not sum up all the concepts of love and, therefore, for centuries it has been in competition with *eros*. If in ancient Greece eros also had the meaning of romantic love as also defined elsewhere (sec. 7), the confusion between these two types has been clearly highlighted.

Furthermore, we can observe that this tendency towards the moral aspect of love is also present in different periods and cultures independently from each other; for instance, in Asian religions and conceptions such as the five noble precepts of Buddhism and the doctrine of Confucianism (see Oldstone-

Moore, 2003, chap. 5), often mixed and confused with aesthetic aspects. Mention should be made of Greco-Roman stoicism (Seneca, 62) and the decisive Kantian ethics (Kant, 1788).

Moreover, a further important consequence stems from this. Just beside the moral evaluation of the emotion (when a feeling is good in the moral sense here promoted) there must also be a psychological and psychiatric one, that is when a feeling is opportune and appropriate. And only in this sense one must deal with *positive* and *negative* feelings-emotions. Otherwise, for this reason, in an aesthetic sense I believe that, as previously mentioned in chapter III, we have to speak of them rather as *beautiful* and *ugly* ones. For instance, if I try to screw in a bolt and am not able, being in a hurry, I try to force it in; the light is dim and I do not see well, therefore, I get angry with everybody around (my wife who does not help me, my son who has left a mess, God who should be omnipresent, etc.). This is a negative emotion since it would be enough to stop, turn on a light, put on my glasses, take the right spanner and everything would go smoothly. How many absurd (negative) emotions arise in our daily life because we do not do things according to a correct procedure or follow the advice of others! However the confusion among the three planes is why the theoretical basis of Positive Psychology (e.g. Fredrickson, 2001, important for the revaluation of "beautiful" emotions) and of human sciences in general is confused and wrong.

Complex concepts

In real life, love is never manifested in a pure way, but always as a mixture of base-types, that are often called by different terms. Two of these complex concepts are so diffused and important, but often misused, that we cannot avoid dealing with them in specific separate discussions.

6) Love as *friendship*

It should be pointed out that in Latin "amicus" has the same root as "amor": friendship or *brotherly love* or *affection among companions* (family, neighbors, schoolmates, co-workers, political party members, church members, adventure companions, etc.). It is a **complex** feeling whose foundations are feelings of desire and love in my sense of the words, that alternate or prevail in every component of a certain group, also having at least one activity in common and some reference values. It is love among relatives, then among individual members of groups based on different ties (places, interests, ideas, sports, amusements, etc.) up to all humanity, as required by Christianity and other religions or ideologies (evident in solidarity in cases of great international disasters and therefore, in theory, reciprocity-exclusivity is not an essential element of it). We are thinking of a tight-knit sports team, without envy among its members, who play united and fairly.

It must be clear that in many languages and cultures and also for many people, today, like centuries ago, defining affection among friends as "love" seems to be exaggerated, shameless and ambiguous as, at least in Italian, the term love is decisively oriented towards a romantic-sexual meaning. Nevertheless, an in-depth analysis leads me to think that these two base feelings, that I have called so, intervene. In everyday life and in the language that one has learnt, everyone calls these situations what he likes best.

As a matter of fact, it is what is called *caritas* in the encyclical of Benedict XVI (2005, sec. 7), in which there is the very important reconciliation of eros and agape, unlike Nygren's thesis (Nygren, 1930). The word *phileo* in ancient Greek predominates for this concept. With regard to contemporary psychology, see the *companionate love* of Grote and Frieze (1994).

Eating together is one of the fundamental signs of friendship.

Finally, I have noticed that friendship has been mainly dealt with by some philosophers in a psychological-ethical sense (Aristotle, 330 BC c.; Cicero, 44 BC; Descartes, 1649; Scheler, 1927), perhaps because the sexual factor is absent.

7) *Romantic* love

Love in the romantic sense is like amicable love, always a mix of the two basic feelings (desire and love), with an added sexual purpose, mediated by wanting to live together (cf. Shaver et al., 1988). Obviously, it is filled with the other beautiful feeling, joy, but often also disappointment, aggressiveness and fear. From these, particular feelings are derived such as *jealousy* (if one fears losing the loved one) or *envy* (if the person belongs to another). It has its specificity in the object, which is restricted to a partner. Therefore, from an aesthetic point of view, the object is not a thing but more: the whole person and, especially, his /her mind ("the heart") because by conquering the mind one also possesses the body in the deepest sense of the word.

Thus, a very intimate state of life is reached to make way for the third essential but consequential aspect: sexuality. Therefore, this type of love can also be called erotic, but now this word has a strong sexual and physical connotation and on the term romantic it seems to me there is a considerable convergence. Indeed, we must point out that there may be a consentient sexuality, a *game* in which a very weak tie is created only to reciprocally satisfy sexual needs without involving romantic love, voluntarily "using" each other's bodies. This is based on the convergence of two desires (in practice, materializing concept 4). Not to mention sex obtained with money (*prostitution*) or with violence (*rape*). In these ways sexuality is never based on love, except for concepts 1, 2 and 4.

On the other hand, romantic love mainly comes true by searching, falling in love with and winning over a partner. All everyday life stories, such as novels, films, etc., produced in various cultures clearly refer to this concept, to these important and overwhelming events that are typical for young people who look for their kindred spirits. Indeed, it always happens in an exclusive couple. A kiss on the mouth is its fundamental sign.

Conjugal love is an even more complex kind of love between two people. About this case in the majority of cultures today, romantic love is also associated with the important moral aspect, the *commitment* to consciously and willingly preserve a relationship. This should be true even when aesthetics goes into crisis: diseases, economic and social difficulties, simple habits, apparently better alternatives, etc.

Furthermore, there is the fundamental commitment to procreate, raise and educate children.

Finally, romantic love has also been used as the maximum METAPHYSICAL symbol: the union of two different cosmic entities should be the key to life and reality (cf. German romanticism, from which the current name is derived).

Conclusion

The first four concepts deal with the *beautiful,* the fifth with the *good.* This is perhaps the most radical and decisive aspect of the research carried out in this chapter.

Thanks to his great philosophical works, Plato became the first philosopher who identified and developed, in a significant way, the concepts of Good (in the wake of Socrates) and Beautiful (in a completely original way), associated with that of love.

However, the enormous prospective capacity of these ideas will require a further very important study that goes beyond neurosciences, and this study, in the context of my theories, should be linked with them in a harmonious and relevant way.

REFERENCES

I. Conditioning

Amsel A. (1992). Confessions of a neobehaviorist, *Integrative Physiological and Behavioral Science*, *4*, 336-346.

Atnip G. W. (1977). Stimulus- and response-reinforcer contingencies in autoshaping, operant, classical, and omission training procedures in rats, *Journal of Experimental Analysis of Behavior*, *28*, 56-69.

Bara B. G. (1990). *Scienza cognitiva*, Bollati Boringhieri, Torino.

Brown P. L. and Jenkins H. M. (1968). Autoshaping of the pigeon's key-peck, *Journal of Experimental Analysis of Behavior*, *11*, 1-8.

Coleman S. R. (1975). Consequences of Response-contingent change in unconditioned stimulus intensity upon the rabbit (*Oryctolagus cuniculus*) nictitating membrane response, *Journal of Comparative and Physiological Psychology*, *88*, 591-595.

Davey G. C. L., Phillips S. and Cleland G. G. (1981). The topography of signal-centered behaviour in the rat: The effects of solid and liquid food reinforcers, *Behaviour Analysis Letters*, *1*, 331-337.

Domjan M. (1993). *The Principles of Learning and Behavior*, Brooks-Cole, Pacific Grove CA.

Garcia J., Ervin F. R. and Koelling R. A. (1966). Learning with prolonged delay of reinforcement, *Psychonomic Science*, *5*, 121-122.

Gormezano I. and Coleman, S. R. (1973). The law of effect and CR contingent modification of the UCS, *Conditional Reflex*, *8*, 41-56.

Hull C. L. (1943). *Principles of behavior*, Appleton-Century-Crofts, New York.

Jenkins H. M., Barnes R. A. and Barrera F. J. (1981). Why autoshaping depends on trial spacing. In: Locurto C. M., Terrace H. S. and Gibbon J. (Eds.), *Autoshaping and conditioning theory*, pp. 255-284, Academic Press, New York.

Kamin L. J. (1968). Attention-like processes in classical conditioning. In: Jones M. R. (Ed.), *Miami symposium on the prediction of behavior: Aversive stimulation*, University of Miami Press, Miami.

Kimble G. A. (1961). *Hilgard and Marquis' conditioning and learning*, Appleton-Century-Crofts, New York.

Lorenz K. (1981). *The foundations of ethology*, Springer-Verlag, Wien.

Mackintosh N. J. (1983). *Conditioning and associative learning*, Oxford University Press, Oxford.

Miller S. and Konorski J. (1928). Sur une forme particuliére des reflexes conditionnels, *Compte rendu hebdomadaire des séances et memoires de la Société de Biologie, 99*, 1155-1157, Paris.

Mowrer O. H. (1947). On the dual nature of learning – a re-interpretation of "conditioning" and "problem-solving", *Harvard Educational Review, 17*, 102-148.

Pavlov I. P. (1927). *Conditioned reflexes*, Oxford University Press, Oxford.

Picker M., Grossett D., Thomas J. and Poling A. (1984). Negative automaintenance: performance of pigeons

under   selective   omission   training   procedure,
Psychological Record, 34, 297-311.

Rescorla R. A. (1988). Pavlovian conditioning - it's not what
you think it is, *American Psychologist, 43,* 151-160.

Rescorla R. A. and Solomon R. L. (1967). Two-process
learning   theory: relationships   between   Pavlovian
conditioning and instrumental learning, *Psychological
Review, 74,* 151-182.

Rescorla R. A. and Wagner A. R. (1972). A theory of Pavlovian
conditioning: Variations   in   the   effectiveness   of
reinforcement and nonreinforcement. In: Black A. H. and
Prokasy W. (Eds), *Classical conditioning II: Current
research and theory,* Appleton-Century-Crofts, New
York.

Seligman M. E. P. and Maier S. F. (1967). Failure to escape
traumatic shock, *Journal of Experimental Psychology, 74,*
1-9.

Seligman M. E. P. (1970). On the generality of the laws of
learning, *Psychological Review, 77,* 406-408.

Shapiro M. M. (1960). Respondent salivary conditioning during
operant lever pressing in dogs, *Science, 132,* 619-620.

Shapiro M. M. and Herendeen D. L. (1975). Food-reinforced
inhibition of conditioned salivation in dogs, *Journal of
Comparative and Physiological Psychology, 88,* 628-632.

Sheffield F. D. (1965). Relation between classical conditioning
and instrumental learning. In: Prokasy W. F. (Ed.),
Classical conditioning: a symposium, pp. 302-322,
Appleton-Century-Crofts, New York.

Skinner B. F. (1935). Two types of conditionned reflex and a
pseudo-type, *Journal of Geneneral Psychology, 12,* 66-
77.

Skinner B. F. (1938). *The behavior of organisms,* Appleton-

Century-Crofts, New York.

Skinner B. F. (1953). *Science and human behavior*, Macmillan, New York.

Spence K. W. (1956). *Behavior Theory and Conditioning*, Yale University Press, New Haven CT.

Staddon J. E. R. (1983). *Adaptive behavior and learning*, Cambridge University Press, Cambridge MT.

Timberlake W. and Lucas G. A. (1989). Behavior systems and learning: From misbehavior to general principles. In: Klein S. B. and Mowrer R. R. (Eds.), *Contemporary learning theories: Instrumental conditioning and the impact of biological constraints on learning*, pp. 237-275, Erlbaum, Hillsdale NJ.

Williams D. R. and Williams H. (1969). Automaintenance in the pigeon: sustained pecking despite contingent non-reinforcement, *Journal of Experimental Analysis of Behavior, 12*, 511-520.

Wyckoff L. B. (1952). The role of observing responses in discrimination learning, *Psychological Review, 59*, 431-442.

Zener K. (1937). The significance of behavior accompanying conditioned salivary secretion for theories of the conditioned Response, *American Journal of Psychology, 50*, 384-403.

II. Behavior

Bard P. (1928). A diencephalic mechanism for the expression of rage with special reference to the sympathetic nervous system, *American Journal of Physiology, 84*, 490-515.

Bower G. H. and Hilgard E. R. (1981). *Theories of learning*, Prentice-Hall, Englewood Cliffs NJ.

Breland K. and Breland M. (1961). The misbehaviour of organisms, *American Psychologist, 16*, 681-684.

Coleman S. R. (1975). Consequences of response-contingent change in unconditioned stimulus intensity upon the rabbit (*Oryctolagus cuniculus*) nictitating membrane response, *Journal of Comparative and Physiological Psychology, 88*, 591-595.

Craig W. (1918). Appetites and Aversions as Constituents of Instincts, *Biological Bulletin, 34*, 91-107.

Finch G. (1938). Salivary conditioning in atropinized dogs, *American Journal Physiology, 124*, 136-141.

Harlow H. F. (1962). The Heterosexual Affectional System in Monkeys, *American Psychologist, 17*, 1-9.

Hill W. (1990). *Learning*, Harper Row, New York.

Hull C. L. (1943). *Principles of behaviour*, Appleton-Century-Crofts, New York.

Johnson-Laird P. N. (1983). *Mental models*, Cambridge University Press, Cambridge UK.

Kohler W. (1927). *The Mentality of Apes*, Kegan-Trench-Trubner, New York.

Konorski J. (1967). *Integrative activity of the brain: An interdisciplinary approach*, University of Chicago Press, Chicago.

Kosslyn S. M. (1983). *Ghosts in the mind's machine: Creating and using images in the brain*, Norton, New York.

Kosslyn S. M. and Koenig O. (1992). *Wet Mind: The New Cognitive Neuroscience*, Macmillian, New York.

Lorenz K. (1981). *The Foundations of Ethology*, Springer-Verlag, New York.

Mackintosh N. J. (1983). *Conditioning and associative learning*, Oxford University Press, Oxford.

Mazur J. E. (1990). *Learning and behaviour*, Prentice-Hall, Englewood Cliffs NJ.

Mowrer O. H. (1947). On the dual nature of learning – A reinterpretation of "conditioning" and "problem-solving", *Harvard Educational Review, 17*, 102-148.

Rescorla R. A. (1988). Pavlovian conditioning - It's not what you think it is, *American Psychologist, 43*, 151-160.

Seligman M. E. P. (1970). On the generality of the laws of learning, *Psychological Review, 77*, 406-418.

Skinner B. F. (1938). *The Behaviour of Organism*, Appleton-Century-Crofts, New York.

Skinner B. F. (1953). *Science and human behaviour*, MacMillian, New York.

Staddon J. E. R. (1983). *Adaptive behaviour and learning*, Cambridge University Press, Cambridge.

Tolman E. C. (1932). *Purposive Behaviour in Animals and Men*, Appleton-Century-Crofts, New York.

Von Bertalanffy L. (1950). The Theory of Open Systems in Physic and Biology, *Science, 111*, 23-29.

Woodworth R. S. (1958). *Dynamics of Behaviour*, Holt-Rinehart-Winston, New York.

Wyckoff L. B. (1952). The role of observing responses in discrimination learning, *Psychological Review, 59*, 431-442.

III. Emotions

Barbalet J. (2004). Hypothesis, Faith, and Commitment: William James' Critique of Science, *Journal for the Theory of Social Behaviour, 34*, 213-230.

Ben-Ze'ev A. (2000). "I Only Have Eyes For You": The Partiality of Positive Emotions, *Journal for the Theory of Social Behaviour, 30*, 341-351.

Berckowitz L. and Harmon-Jones E. (2004). Toward an Understanding of the Determinants of Anger, *Emotion, 4*, 107-130.

Cannon W. B. (1929). *Bodily Changes in Panic, Hunger, Fear and Rage*, Appleton-Century, New York.

Damasio A. R. (1999). *The feeling of what happens: Body and emotion in the making of consciousness*, Harcourt Brace, New York.

Davidson R. J., Scherer K. R. and Goldsmith H. H. (Eds.) (2003). *Handbook of affective sciences*, Oxford University Press, New York.

Djikic M. and Oatley K. (2004). Love and Personal Relationships: Navigating on the Border Between the Ideal and the Real, *Journal for the Theory of Social Behaviour, 34*, 199-209.

Ekman P. (1982). *Emotion in the Human Face*, Cambridge University Press, Cambridge.

Ellsworth P. C. (1994). William James and Emotion: Is a Century of Fame Worth a Century of Misunderstanding? *Psychological Review, 2*, 222-229.

Fredrickson B. L. (2004). The broaden-and-build theory of positive emotions, *Philosophical Transactions of the Royal Society of London / Series B – Biological Science, 359*, 1367-1377.

Frijda N. H. (1994). Emotions are functional, Most of the time. In: Eckman P. and Davidson R. J. (Eds.), *The nature of emotion: fundamental questions,* pp. 112-122, Oxford University Press, New York.

Frijda N. H. (2004). Emotions and Action. In: Manstead A. S. R., Frijda N. H. and Fischer A. (Eds.), *Feeling and Emotions – The Amsterdam Symposium,* p. 171, Cambridge University Press, Cambridge.

Izard C. E. (1990). The Substrates and Functions of Emotions and Feelings: William James and Current Emotion Theory, *Personality and Social Psychology Bulletin, 16,* 626-635.

James W. (1884). What is an emotion? *Mind, 9,* 188-205.

Johnson-Laird P. N. and Oatley K. (1989). The Language of Emotions: An Analysis of a Semantic Field, *Cognition and Emotion, 3,* 81-123.

Lazarus R. S. (1991). Progress on a cognitive-motivational-relational theory of emotion, *American Psychologist, 46,* 819-834.

Panksepp J. (1998). *Affective neuroscience,* Oxford University Press, New York.

Royzman E. B. and Sabini J. (2001). Something it Takes to be an Emotion: The Interesting Case of Disgust, *Journal for the Theory of Social Behaviour, 31,* 29-59.

Sabini J. and Silver M. (2005). Ekman's basic emotions: Why not love and jealousy? *Cognition and emotion, 19,* 693-712.

Schachter S. and Singer J. E. (1962). Cognitive, social and physiological determinants of emotional state, *Psychological Review, 69,* 379-399.

Scherer K. R. (2000). Emotion. In: Hewstone M. and Stroebe W. (Eds.), *Introduction to social psychology: A European perspective,* Blackwell, Oxford.

Schorr A. (2001). Appraisal: The Evolution of an Idea. In Scherer K. R., Schor A. and Johnstone T. (Eds.), *AppraisalProcesses in Emotion – Theory, Methods, Research,* pp. 20-34, Oxford University Press, New York.

Silvia P. J. (2005). What is Interesting? Exploring the Appraisal Structure of Interest. *Emotion, 5,* 89-102.

Solomon R. C. (2002). Back to the Basics: On the Very Idea of "Basic Emotions", *Journal for the Theory of Social Behaviour, 32,* 115-144.

Solomon R. C. and Stone L. D. (2002). On "Positive" and "Negative" Emotions, *Journal for the Theory of Social Behaviour, 32,* 417-435.

IV. Love

Aristotle (330 BC c.). *Etica Nicomachea,* Laterza, Bari 2007

Benedict XVI (2005). Encyclical letter *Deus caritas est,* www.vatican.va.

Berscheid E. (2010). Love in the Fourth Dimension, *Annual Review of Psychology, 61,* 1-25.

Bowlby J. (1969). *Attachment and Loss,* Basic Books, New York.

Cicero (44 BC). *Laelius de amicitia.*

Descartes R. (1649). Le passioni dell'anima, Bompiani, Milano. Or. ed: *Les passions de l'âme.*

Dessler E. E. (1930 c.). *Michtav me Eliyahu,* Vol. 1.

Empedocles (460 BC c.). *Purificationes,* Tonelli A. (Ed.), Bompiani, Milano 2002.

Fehr B., Sprecher S. and Underwood L. G. (Eds.) (2009). *The science of compassionate love,* Wiley-Blackwell, Chichester UK.

Fredrickson B. L. (2001). The role of Positive Emotions in Positive Psychology, *American Psychologist, 56,* 218-226.

Freud S. (1920). *Al di là del principio del piacere,* Mondadori, Milano 2007. Or. ed.: *Jenseits des Lustprinzips.*

Grote N. K. and Frieze I. H. (1994). The measurement of friendship-based love in intimate relationship, *Personal Relationships, 1,* 275-300.

Kant I. (1788). *Critica della ragion pratica ed altri scritti morali,* UTET, Torino 1995. Or. ed.: *Kritik der praktischen Vernunft,* Hartknoch, Riga.

Nygren A. (1930). *Eros e agape: La nozione cristiana dell'amore,* EDB, Bologna 1990. Or. ed.: *Agape and Eros: the Christian Idea of Love,* University of Chicago

Press, Chicago.

Oldstone-Moore J. (2003). *Understanding confucianism*, Duncan Baird Publishers.

Plato (400 BC c.). *Simposio,* Laterza, Bari 1996.

Seneca L. A. j. (62) *De beneficiis.*

Shaver P. R., Hazan C. and Bradshaw D. (1988). Love as attachment: The integration of three behavioral systems. In: Sterneberg R. J. and Barnes M. (Eds.), *The psychology of Love,* pp. 68-99, Yale University Press, New Haven.

Scheler M. (1927). *Il formalismo nell'etica e l'etica materiale dei valori,* San Paolo, Milano 1996. Or. ed. *Der Formalismus in der Ethik und die materiale Wertethik,* Verlag, Halle.

Schopenhauer A. (1819). *Il mondo come volontà e rappresentazione.* Or. ed.: *Die welt als Wille und Vorstellung,* Leipzig.

Sternberg R. J. (1986). A Triangular Theory of Love, *Psychological Review, 93,* 119-135.

Sternberg R. J. (1987). Liking Versus Loving: A Comparative Evaluation of Theories, *Psichological Bullettin, 102,* 331-345.